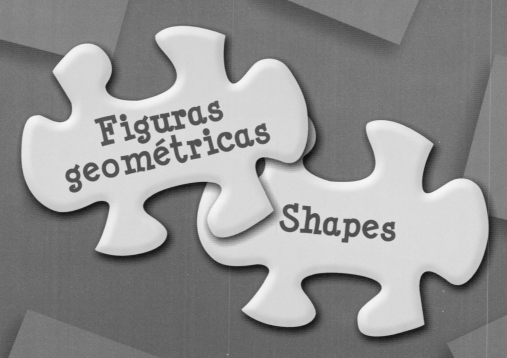

Figuras geométricas

Shapes

Cuadrados/Squares

por/by Sarah L. Schuette

Traducción/Translation: Dr. Martín Luis Guzmán Ferrer

Asesora literaria/Reading Consultant:

Dra. Elena Bodrova, asesora principal/Senior Consultant

Mid-continent Research for Education and Learning

A+ books
BILINGÜE/BILINGUAL

CAPSTONE PRESS
a capstone imprint

A+ Books are published by Capstone Press,
151 Good Counsel Drive, P.O. Box 669, Mankato, Minnesota 56002.
www.capstonepress.com

Books published by Capstone Press are manufactured with
paper containing at least 10 percent post-consumer waste.

Library of Congress Cataloging-in-Publication Data
Schuette, Sarah L., 1976–
    [Squares. Spanish & English]
    Cuadrados : cuadrados a nuestro alrededor = Squares : seeing squares all around us /
por Sarah L. Schuette
    p. cm. — (A+ bilingüe. Figuras geométricas = A+ bilingual. Shapes)
    Summary: "Simple text, photographs, and illustrations show squares in everyday objects — in both
English and Spanish" — Provided by publisher.
    Includes index.
    ISBN 978-1-4296-4588-1 (lib. bdg.)
    1. Square — Juvenile literature. I. Title. II. Title: Squares : seeing squares all around us. III. Series.
QA482.S38218 2010
516'.154 — dc22   2009040928

Created by the A+ Team

Sarah L. Schuette, editor; Katy Kudela, bilingual editor; Adalin Torres-Zayas, Spanish copy editor;
    Heather Kindseth, art director and designer; Jason Knudson, designer and illustrator;
    Angi Gahler, illustrator; Gary Sundermeyer, photographer; Nancy White, photo stylist;
    Eric Manske, production specialist

Note to Parents, Teachers, and Librarians
The Figuras geométricas/Shapes series uses color photographs and a nonfiction format to introduce
children to the shapes around them in both English and Spanish. It is designed to be read aloud
to a pre-reader or to be read independently by an early reader. The images help early readers and
listeners understand the text and concepts discussed. The book encourages further learning by
including the following: Table of Contents, Glossary, Internet Sites, and Index. Early readers may
need assistance using these features.

Table of Contents/
Tabla de contenidos

Squares are shapes with four sides all the same.

Los cuadrados son formas con cuatro lados todos del mismo tamaño.

5

A board for chess or
checkers has 64 squares.
Each game piece sits on
a square. Players move the
pieces to different squares.

El tablero del ajedrez o de
damas tiene 64 cuadrados.
En cada juego las piezas se
colocan en uno de los cuadrados.
Los jugadores mueven las piezas
a los diferentes cuadrados.

A board of squares
can make a game.

Un tablero de
cuadros puede formar
un juego de mesa.

7

A sandbox square is where you play.

Un arenero cuadrado es un lugar donde puedes jugar.

9

What Squares Do/
Qué es lo que hacen
los cuadrados

FEBRUARY

Monday	Monday	Tuesday	Wednesday	Thursday	Friday	Satu
						6
				5	
			4		13
		3		12	
	2		11		
1		10		19	
	9		18		
8		17		26	
	16		25		
15		24		

10

Squares tell you the month and day.

. . . .

Los cuadrados te dicen el mes y el día.

y

7

14

21

28

27

©TREND

A square can wrap
around your head.

. . . .

Tú puedes envolverte la
cabeza con un cuadrado.

14

A square can be a slice of bread.

. . . .

El cuadrado puede ser una rebanada de pan.

Quilters sew squares of cloth together to make a quilt. Quilts are warm covers on cold nights.

Las costureras cosen cuadrados de tela para hacer un edredón. Los edredones son cobertores calientes para noches frías.

Slip under these squares and take a nap.

Métete bajo estos cuadrados para dormir la siesta.

It is a good thing that we have napkins. Long ago, people wiped their dirty hands on their clothes.

Es bueno que nosotros tengamos servilletas. Hace mucho, las personas se limpiaban las manos sucias en su ropa.

At dinner you keep this square on your lap.

En la cena tú te pones este cuadrado sobre las piernas.

19

20

Some tables are covered with squares when we eat.

Algunas mesas están cubiertas de cuadrados cuando comemos.

Square tiles decorate the floors of many homes. Some tiles are made out of clay. Clay tiles are baked in a kiln. A kiln is a very hot oven.

Las losetas cuadradas adornan los pisos de muchas casas. Algunas losetas están hechas de barro. Las losetas de barro se cuecen en hornazas. Una hornaza en un horno muy caliente.

Small squares are floor tiles under your feet.

Las losetas del piso bajo tus pies son pequeños cuadrados.

23

Sarah Square
123 Square Ave. S.
Squareville, S. D.
54321

A colorful square helps hold your letter.

Un cuadrado muy colorido sirve para guardar tu carta.

Which of these shapes
do you know better?

¿Cuál de todas estas formas conoces mejor?

Play Marshmallow Squares/
Juega al cuadrado de malvaviscos

You will need/Necesitas:

1 box of colored toothpicks/una caja de palillos de colores

1 bag of small marshmallows/ una bolsa de malvaviscos chicos

1 bag of large marshmallows/una bolsa de malvaviscos grandes

1 Connect four small marshmallows with four toothpicks to make a square.

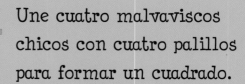

1 Une cuatro malvaviscos chicos con cuatro palillos para formar un cuadrado.

28

2 Push another toothpick into one marshmallow in your square and build another square. Keep building until you have four squares across.

3 Now, build the squares going up until you have four rows of four.

4 Place one large marshmallow into each square except one. Pick one marshmallow and jump over another marshmallow to land in the empty square. Remove the marshmallow that you jumped. You can skip around the board, picking different marshmallows to jump. Can you jump all of the marshmallows and only have one left on the board?

2 Mete otro palillo en uno de tus cuadrados y forma otro cuadrado. Continúa formándolos hasta que tengas cuatro cuadrados a lo largo.

3 Ahora, forma cuadrados para arriba hasta que tengas cuatro filas de cuatro.

4 Coloca un malvavisco grande en cada uno de los cuadrados excepto en uno. Toma uno de los malvaviscos grandes y salta sobre otro malvavisco para llegar al cuadrado vacío. Quita los malvaviscos que vas saltando. Puedes brincar por todo el tablero, escogiendo los malvaviscos que quieres saltar. ¿Puedes saltar todos los malvaviscos hasta que sólo haya uno en el tablero?

29

Glossary

clay — a type of earth that can be shaped and baked to make bricks, pottery, and tile

decorate — to add things to a room or an object to make it look nice

kiln — a very hot oven that is used to bake objects made out of clay; the objects are baked until the clay is hard and dry.

napkin — a square piece of paper or cloth used to protect your clothing when you eat

quilt — a warm blanket; some quilts are made of square pieces of cloth called quilt blocks that are sewn together in a pattern.

tile — a square piece of stone, plastic, or baked clay; people put tiles on floors and walls; they can arrange the tiles to make pictures or patterns.

Internet Sites

FactHound offers a safe, fun way to find Internet sites related to this book. All of the sites on FactHound have been researched by our staff.

Here's all you do:

Visit *www.facthound.com*

30

FactHound will fetch the best sites for you!

Glosario

adornar — añadir cosas a una habitación u objeto para que se vea bonito

el barro — tipo de tierra a la que puede dársele forma y cocerse para hacer ladrillos, alfarería y losetas

el edredón — cobertor caliente; algunos cobertores están hechos de piezas de tela que se llaman bloques y se cosen uno a otro formando un diseño.

la hornaza — horno muy caliente que se usa para cocer objetos hechos de barro; los objetos se cuecen hasta que el barro queda duro y seco.

la loseta — pieza cuadrada de piedra, plástico o barro cocido; las personas ponen loseta en pisos y paredes; se pueden arreglar las losetas formando cuadros o diseños.

la servilleta — cuadrado de papel o tela que se usa para proteger tu ropa cuando comes

Sitios de Internet

FactHound brinda una forma segura y divertida de encontrar sitios de Internet relacionados con este libro. Todos los sitios en FactHound han sido investigados por nuestro personal.

Esto es todo lo que tú necesitas hacer:

Visita *www.facthound.com*

¡FactHound buscará los mejores sitios para ti!

Index

Índice